Facebook For Business Owners

FACEBOOK MARKETING FOR FAN PAGE OWNERS AND SMALL BUSINESSES

TOM CORSON-KNOWLES

Get more online marketing tips and strategies in the newsletter for free at <u>BlogBusinessSchool.com</u>

Typeset in Cambria. Used with permission from Microsoft.

EARNINGS DISCLAIMER

When addressing financial matters in any of books, sites, videos, newsletters or other content, we've taken every effort to ensure we accurately represent our products and services and their ability to improve your life or grow your business. However, there is no guarantee that you will get any results or earn any money using any of our ideas, tools, strategies or recommendations, and we do not purport any "get rich schemes" in any of our content. Nothing in this book is a promise or guarantee of earnings. Your level of success in attaining similar results is dependent upon a number of factors including your skill, knowledge, ability, dedication, business savvy, network, and financial situation, to name a few. Because these factors differ according to individuals, we cannot and do not guarantee your success, income level, or ability to earn revenue. You alone are responsible for your actions and results in life and business. Any forward-looking statements outlined in this book or on our Sites are simply our opinion and thus are not guarantees or promises for actual performance. It should be clear to you that by law we make no guarantees that you will achieve any results from our ideas or models presented in this book or on our Sites, and we offer no professional legal, medical, psychological or financial advice.

WHY I WROTE THIS BOOK

CRISO

I WAS a college student when Facebook first came out. I thought it was cool. Little did I know that it would be earning me thousands of dollars a month for my online business in just a few short years.

Having been on Facebook for eight years and seen its evolution and change first-hand, I've got some experience with it. But it wasn't until the end of 2007 when Facebook announced Fan Pages that I really saw the potential for massive profits from Facebook.

Since then, I've spent tens of thousands of dollars on every Facebook marketing training course out there and thousands more on Facebook Ads.

I've finally created a simple system that anyone can use to grow their business online using Facebook – for free or at very low cost using Facebook Ads.

Get more free Facebook and online marketing tips in the newsletter at:

www.BlogBusinessSchool.com

WHY YOU SHOULD READ THIS BOOK

☙❧

ARE YOU as excited about using Facebook to grow your business as I am?

If not, there can only be a few reasons why:

1) You're not currently using Facebook. If that's the case, then this book will probably change your life.

2) You use Facebook but think it's just a waste of time because you're not getting any new customers from it. If that's you then you will LOVE chapter 5 where you will learn the step-by-step system that creates new leads every day from Facebook.

3) You've read other books about Facebook or even taken courses on how to grow your business on Facebook but you're still not getting the results you would like to see. If that's you then I want to make you a special promise.

If you finish reading this book and apply what it teaches and you're not amazed by the incredible improvements in your Facebook marketing results, just contact me at ***tom@juicetom.com*** and I will refund your purchase price of this book.

This book will help you grow your business using Facebook – I guarantee it!

TABLE OF CONTENTS

൬ൈ

CHAPTER 1:
FACEBOOK MARKETING STRATEGY – THE WHY

ᲝᲳᲒᲒᲐ

THIS CHAPTER is all about WHY: Why use Facebook for your business? Why do over 1 billion people use Facebook on a regular basis? Why is Facebook the best option in the entire world of HIGHLY TARGETED advertising campaigns? Why is every single Fortune 500 company in the world actively marketing their business on Facebook? Why are online marketers (like me) raving about Facebook's potential for growing a small business?

But even more importantly... why is it worth your time to learn how to use Facebook in the first place?

Let me answer this most important question first. You see, I believe it's worth your time to learn how to use Facebook because it is THE MEDIA of today and tomorrow.

You see, in the past the media was television, newspapers and radio. Big companies would spend big advertising budgets on ads in each of these forms of media and, for the most part, these campaigns would be profitable.

Today, everything has changed...

NEWSPAPER ADVERTISING AND MARKETING

Newspapers are going out of business left and right. Heck, people are wondering if the New York Times, the most prestigious Newspaper business in the world, will go out of business (and for good reason – they are certainly in financial trouble).

The newspaper business is in serious trouble. It's dying. It's changing. It probably won't be around much longer, and if it does continue, it won't continue in the same way – things will have to change. It's become virtually impossible to create or sustain a profitable newspaper business in the new age of media where the internet is king and newspapers are old news.

But with the dying newspaper industry, can't you get some screaming hot deals on newspaper ads? I mean, it's always easier to negotiate with companies that are in financial trouble, right?

Well, yes, that's true... you can probably negotiate a better deal now on newspaper ads than ever before in the history of the world – but do you really want to invest your time, money, energy and effort in learning how to master advertising in a media that is dying?

I know I don't! If I'm going to master advertising, I want to do it in a media that is growing or at least staying stable and has a good chance of lasting. Why spend all that time and energy learning something that might not even be useful in a few years?

I have a feeling that this internet thing isn't going away. I mean, people aren't going to wake up someday and say, "You know what, instead of reading about today's news today, I'd like to wait and read about it tomorrow in a newspaper – and while I'm at it, I'd like to pay for that privilege of seeing the news a day late as well." Not gonna happen!

Now, certainly, there are similarities between advertising in all media – and you can often apply lessons from one type of ad to another type. But if you're going to build a successful business, you need to become a master at advertising and marketing – not just a dabbler. Why not master the important stuff?

I think the internet and Facebook are important media and they will remain important for a long time.

RADIO ADVERTISING AND MARKETING

Radio, too, is a dying industry. It's certainly not as bad as the newspaper industry, but it is changing rapidly.

Today, anyone can create a radio show. It's called a podcast show or internet radio show and there are millions of them. In fact, I have two internet radio shows myself with thousands of loyal listeners.

And how much did it cost me to attract thousands of loyal listeners to my internet radio show? About $20 a month for hosting. Not a bad investment.

Compare that with radio advertising where you could easily burn through $2,000 a month and still not be sure if it's actually creating new sales for you.

Radio is dying for a number of reasons. Internet radio shows like mine are certainly a reason – more and more people are tuning into internet radio and podcasts to learn more about the subjects they're interested in or to listen to the type of music they want to without interruptions from advertisers.

Then there's Sirius and XM radio and they've changed the whole game. Instead of listening to ads and just a few radio stations in your car, you can pay a subscription and get a virtually unlimited selection of radio and avoid all the ads.

There's also the whole smartphone and iPod revolution. I see more people listening to their iPods in their car than people who still listen to the radio. And why wouldn't they?

Honestly, if you had the choice of taking a chance with radio music vs. playing your own favorite songs whenever you wanted, which would you choose?

You see, today is the age of modern media. And modern media is all about consumer choice. Consumers want instant access to what they want. They don't want commercial breaks or yesterday's news. They don't want to listen to country when what they really love to hear is jazz. Everything's changed.

And Facebook is a huge part of that change as you will soon see...

Television Advertising and Marketing

Although some bloggers say the television industry is dying, I don't agree with them. The television industry is certainly changing but I don't think it's dying (yet).

There are still over 100 million cable TV subscribers in the United States and last time I checked the average American was still watching 4 hours of TV a day.

But the industry is definitely changing! Now with TiVo, consumers can never watch a commercial again – and they love that idea!

Although television advertising is still big business, it's not profitable for 99% of small businesses. Don't believe me? Go blow $10,000 on a small TV spot and let me know how much profit you make on that deal.

Some people say it's internet TV that's killing television but I'm not sure I agree. Sure, YouTube is awesome and so are Netflix and other services online.

But when it comes to YouTube shows vs. Television shows, there's still a huge gap in quality. This gap is quickly shrinking, however, with more independent online videographers learning about newer, cheaper and more efficient ways to create high quality video online.

The fact of the matter is this: If you want to advertise your small business and have a choice between television and YouTube, YouTube is far better!

First of all, you can test much easier with YouTube. Creating a YouTube video for promoting your business can be done with the iPhone or other smart phone you probably already have (or just borrow your friends' phone!)

Then, you can promote it with some simple YouTube ads or even Facebook ads. By the time you've spent $100 on ads for that video, you will already know whether or not it's a profitable advertising campaign.

Compare that to traditional TV advertising where it's probably going to cost you a few thousand dollars JUST to create the video for your spot. Then, air time is going to cost you a lot more.

Which risk would you rather take? Big risk or small risk?

If you're a savvy entrepreneur, you'd rather test the smaller risk first. I don't know about you but I'd rather take a small risk and then scale up once it's profitable rather than take a big risk and hope that I get rich before I go broke. How about you?

Facebook Advertising and Marketing

Compare the online media industry with radio, newspaper and TV and you'll see it's the only one that's growing (and growing rapidly!).

There are so many reasons why...

Consumers love the speed of information on the internet. They get today's news today. They get hot deals on penny auction sites and eBay. They get cheaper books on Amazon. They get more movies faster on Netflix with no late fees (and now Amazon Instant Video which is huge!). They stay in touch with their friends on Facebook and Twitter.

For consumers the internet is a HUGE win over traditional media.

But I think it's an even bigger win for entrepreneurs like you and me!

Just as the internet has dramatically reduced the cost of buying books, reading news, watching movies and staying in touch with friends, it's also reduced the cost of doing business – so much so that anyone anywhere in the world can start a business online if they have the a computer and internet access.

In fact, if you have an internet connection and a computer, you don't even need ONE PENNY to start an online business!

There are millions of sites like Blogger, Wordpress, YouTube, Facebook, Twitter and Squidoo that will host your content for you for free, no problem.

Then there are millions of product owners who will let you sell their products for commission in what are called affiliate programs, no problem.

So with just a little bit of work you can create a business website for free, hosted by someone else, and sell someone else's product for commissions to earn revenue.

This is just one example of a way to start your own business online without spending a penny. There are a million more ways to do it – the only limit is the current technological breakthroughs we have and your creativity.

I'm not saying I think it's best to start a business online or market your current business online without spending a penny. I think there are some wise investments you ought to make in marketing your business online. But the fact of the matter is that you will never need to spend nearly as much as entrepreneurs had to just 20 years ago.

Okay, so you'll need to spend a few hundred dollars on graphic design and maybe web design. Maybe you'll need video hosting software or this and that. Total expenditures? A few thousand dollars probably. You can get by with much less (I know I did when I first started!).

My point is this – there's never been an easier time to start a business than today. And there's never been an easier time to grow a business than today thanks to the internet. Everything has changed.

And nowhere is that more apparent than with Facebook itself. This little company started in the dorm room of some guy who couldn't get a girlfriend in 2004. Today, the company is worth billions. It's an unbelievable story!

But what's even more unbelievable about it is what it's doing for small business owners like me and you...

Now thanks to Facebook you can connect with your target customers – for free!

Now thanks to Facebook you can stay in touch with your past customers and offer them DAILY tips, advice, information, discounts, deals and much more – for free!

Now thanks to Facebook you can find out what problems your potential customers are having RIGHT WHEN THEY HAVE THE PROBLEM – and connect with them and help them solve that problem – for free!

Now thanks to Facebook you can have your customers spread your message and your marketing to thousands of their friends at the click of a button – for free!

Now thanks to Facebook you can run the most highly targeted advertising campaigns in the history of the world – for just a few cents a click.

Facebook has changed everything for small business owners. Let me show you how to profit from this change.

CHAPTER 2:
GETTING STARTED WITH FACEBOOK – YOUR PERSONAL PROFILE

C3¥80

O KAY, THIS chapter is for those of you who are brand new to Facebook. If you already have a personal profile, you can skip this chapter (although you may find the section on your Timeline cover *photos to be quite useful).*

HOW TO SETUP YOUR PERSONAL FACEBOOK PROFILE

STEP 1. GO TO FACEBOOK.COM

Sign Up
It's free and always will be.

First Name	Last Name

Your Email

Re-enter Email

New Password

STEP 2. FILL IN YOUR INFO

You will need to fill in your first and last name, email, password, sex and birthday to join Facebook.

STEP 3. INVITE YOUR FRIENDS TO CONNECT

Next, Facebook will ask you to connect with your friends who are already on Facebook. To do so, simply pick your email service you use and login with that password – Facebook will automatically show you all your friends who you've emailed that are already on Facebook and you can add them all with the click of a button.

Note: Unless you are a celebrity or extremely well-known, I HIGHLY recommend you add everyone you know as a friend on Facebook. This will dramatically increase the size of your network and help you in your online marketing efforts.

You never know how big a difference just one person could make! Treasure each of those connections.

STEP 4. FILL IN YOUR EDUCATION & WORK INFO

Next, just fill in your high school, college and current employer information (it's okay to leave it blank if you didn't graduate from college or what not). I highly recommend filling out this info so that you can connect with past schoolmates and your co-workers.

Again, this will increase the size of your network and help you in your marketing efforts.

STEP 5. UPLOAD A PROFILE PICTURE

Next, Facebook will ask you to upload a picture of yourself. It's best to get a headshot of you. If not, any photo of you that will be recognizable to your friends will do.

I highly recommend putting a photo of yourself on your profile! You'll see some people who put photos of their children, pets or some random picture there – I DO NOT recommend that. It looks VERY unprofessional and will not help you in your marketing efforts.

STEP 6. POST A STATUS UPDATE AND CELEBRATE!

Next, it's time to post your first "status update" on Facebook. This is a public message that your friends will be able to see when they login to Facebook or look at your profile.

The very next page after uploading your profile picture is called your "Newsfeed" or your personal Facebook Home page. In the middle, you will see photos, videos and text updates from your friends.

At the top in the middle there is a small box that says "What's on your mind?"

Click in that box and you can type in your first status update on Facebook – anything will do!

If you don't know what to type just copy and paste this,

"This is my first status update on Facebook! Thanks to Facebook For Business Owners I'm finally on Facebook!"

Update Status   **Add Photos/Video**

What's on your mind?

ADVANCED PROFILE SETUP

Okay, now you've set up your personal profile, connected with your friends and posted your first status update! Good for you!

Next, it's time for some advanced profile setup. I recommend you do this advanced work as soon as you can but it's not 100% necessary to do right away.

This advanced setup will help make your profile look more complete and professional and aid you in marketing your business online (which is what this book is all about!).

So let's get to work!

STEP 1. UPLOAD A TIMELINE COVER PHOTO

Facebook now gives you two photos on your profile page. The first, which you've already uploaded, is called your Facebook Profile Picture. The second is your Facebook Timeline Cover Photo.

When you login to Facebook and see your newsfeed (home page), there are two places you can click to access your profile page. 1) Click your name or picture on the top left of the screen or 2) click your name or picture on the top right of the screen.

Once you've clicked your name/photo, you should see your profile page. It should look like this (except yours will be a bit more empty looking):

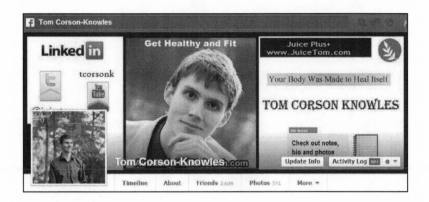

The large image that takes up most of the top of your profile page is the Timeline Cover Photo. Yours should be blank. To edit it, simply scroll over that empty space and you will see a button that says, "Change Cover" – Scroll over that and click "Upload a Photo." Then, you can upload your Timeline Cover Photo.

Note: Your Timeline Cover Photo area size is 851 pixels wide x 315 pixels tall. It's okay if your picture is bigger than that because Facebook will crop it for you.

What kind of cover photo should you upload?

There are all kinds of cover photos you can upload. If your primary goal is to market your business, then uploading a photo that **brands** you is a good idea. For example, if you're a dog groomer, your Timeline cover photo could include a picture of a dog getting a beautiful groom and maybe a tagline as well that says "New England's #1 Dog Groomer!"

You can always change your cover photo and profile picture later so don't worry about being perfect right now!

Note: If you need someone to design the graphics for you for your cover photo, try using ***www.Fiverr.com*** where you can find someone to do it for you for just $5!

STEP 2. UPDATE YOUR PROFILE INFORMATION

The next thing you should do is update your info on your profile. To do that, click the "Update Info" button to the right of your name just under your Timeline Cover Photo.

Once you click Update Info, you should see a page that looks like this.

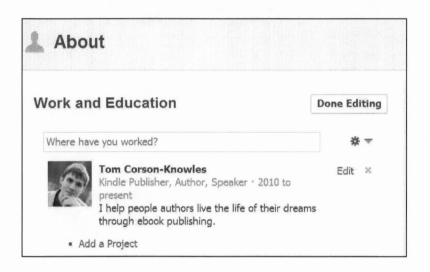

On this page, you can add any jobs you've had or currently have and any education you've received from pre-schools to universities. I recommend adding your current job or business, your high school and college to your profile. This will help you connect with colleagues, promote your current business/job and connect with classmates from high school and college.

Next, you can write a bit more about yourself in the "About You" section. I recommend just writing at least a few sentences to let people know who you are and what you're up to in life.

Next, you can edit your "Living" section to include your hometown and your current city you're living in – this will help make local connections for you and your business.

Next, you can edit your "Basic Info" including any languages you speak, religious views and political views.

Next, you can edit your "Contact Info" – make SURE to include your website for your business here as well as any other websites you would like to list. Also list a phone number (just visible to your friends on Facebook) and an email!

I can't tell you how many times I've wanted to contact someone on Facebook to do business with them and they didn't have their contact info – so I decided to work with someone else instead. Don't let that happen to you!

Finally, you can edit your "Favorite Quotations" section by adding any of your favorite quotes that you'd like to feature on your profile.

> *"All hard work brings a profit,*
> *but mere talk leads only to poverty."*
>
> **Proverbs 14:23**

Congratulations! You've completed the hard work of filling out your profile on Facebook completely. Now let's get to the good stuff – how to market your business on Facebook using a Facebook Fan Page.

CHAPTER 3
HOW FACEBOOK WORKS

 C3&C)

A T THIS point, I think it's important you get an understanding of how Facebook works before we move on to creating a fan page.

Make sure you've completed your personal profile, added friends on Facebook and have posted at least one status update so that you'll be able to understand all of this information by navigating your own Facebook pages.

STATUS UPDATES

Status updates are the "bread and butter" of Facebook. Status updates are what makes Facebook interesting, fascinating and new every single day.

Any person with a profile or fan page can post a status update and many people post several times a day.

Status updates can include just plain text, a photo (with or without text), a video (with or without text) or a link to another website (with or without text).

Status updates can also include "Places" which are physical places one might visit (like Ocean World, for example or a restaurant).

Status updates can also include "Life Events" which can be anything from publishing a book (like this one) to getting married to starting a hobby (there are hundreds of life events you can add to Facebook).

Status updates are how you share information on Facebook and anyone who visits your profile can see your status updates (although you can edit your Privacy Settings on Facebook to change it so that only your friends can see your status updates but I do not recommend this for marketing).

In addition, your personal status updates can be seen through your friends' news feeds.

FACEBOOK NEWS FEED

The Facebook news feed is basically a live news feed to all of your Facebook friends (and fan pages that you've liked and groups you are a member of).

Every time you post a status update, it will appear in your friends' news feed (assuming they are online near the time you posted it and they are subscribed to your status updates).

LIKING, COMMENTING AND SHARING

Anyone on Facebook (again, depending on your privacy settings) can like, comment or share any of your status updates.

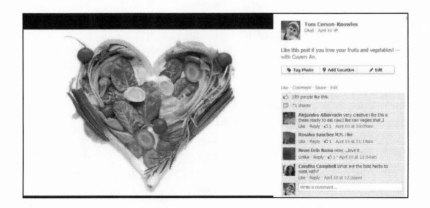

In the screenshot above, you can see one of my status updates which is just a picture. The picture received 189 likes, 70 shares and 4 comments.

A "Like" is basically like a vote saying you liked the post and you think your friends might like it too. Every time you like a status update, it is more likely to be seen by your friends.

A "Comment" is literally a comment you can write underneath every status update to join the conversation.

A "Share" is when you click the share button and that status update now gets posted to your profile (so if you clicked share on the picture above, you would then be posting that photo on your own profile as a brand new status update).

In terms of marketing and exposure, shares will get your more exposure in other peoples' news feeds than comments which will get your more exposure than likes.

Shares > Comments > Likes

This doesn't mean likes and comments aren't good – they're great! You want as many shares, comments and likes as you can get to help expand your marketing reach.

EdgeRank – The Algorithm (Important!)

EdgeRank is Facebook's secret algorithm for determining how many people will see your status updates. For example, the average Fan Page status update is only seen by 16% of fans. So if you have 10,000 fans on your Facebook fan page and your page has an average EdgeRank, only 1600 fans will see you average post.

So what's the key to more exposure on Facebook? Increase your EdgeRank!

How does EdgeRank work?

No one knows the algorithm for EdgeRank (and it probably changes regularly like Google's search results algorithm) but there are a few things we know for sure:

1) The more comments, likes and shares your status updates receive, the higher your EdgeRank will be.

2) If people ignore your status updates, it will lower your EdgeRank.

So the key for improving your EdgeRank is to post content that is interesting and engaging. It's got to be content that other people WANT to share, like and comment on.

Thus, Facebook is rewarding quality – the better quality your posts, the better engagement you will receive, the higher your EdgeRank will be and the more people you will reach with your message.

This is why many marketers fail on Facebook because they ignore EdgeRank. Rather than posting useful content for their fans and friends, they just post sales offers that bore people away so they get no likes, shares or comments and their EdgeRank falls off a cliff.

Don't let that happen to you!

Some of the biggest mistakes people make that damage their EdgeRank include:

1) Posting too many sales offers or being too pushy.
2) Not posting a variety of content (you want to post lots of photos, videos, text and links not just all links).
3) Buying Facebook Fans (this is not only against Facebook's Terms of Service agreement but it will also destroy your EdgeRank).
4) Getting fans who don't care about your content (This often happens if you use Facebook ads or another way to attract fans

from other countries or who are not interested in your business).

ALWAYS REMEMBER

The key to increasing your EdgeRank is to post engaging content that gets people to like, share and comment.

Now that you understand EdgeRank, you know more than 99% of other business owners who are on Facebook! So good for you!

Now let's get you a fan page!

CHAPTER 4
SETTING UP YOUR BUSINESS WITH A FACEBOOK FAN PAGE

CR20

N OW IT'S time to create a Facebook Fan Page. Make sure you've at least followed the basic profile setup for your Facebook Profile in Chapter 2 because you can't create a Fan Page without a Facebook Profile setup.

WHAT IS A FACEBOOK FAN PAGE?

Facebook Fan Pages were introduced in late 2007 as a way to help businesses connect with customers on Facebook. Previously, Facebook had noticed that a lot of users (like me) had been marketing their business using their personal profile – and Facebook wanted to separate the business aspects of the site from the friendship and connection.

So they created fan pages which are basically a profile page for a business (although there are several major differences as you will soon see).

HOW TO CREATE A FACEBOOK FAN PAGE

STEP 1

Go to *www.facebook.com/pages* and click "Create your own" on the top right of the page.

STEP 2

Pick your type of Fan Page that best relates to your business. If you're a local business, pick "Local Business or Place." Just try your best to pick the type of fan page that matches your business but don't worry about it too much because Facebook allows you to change it after your page is set up.

After you pick the business type, you will need to fill in some basic info about your business and pick your Business Name which will become the name of your fan page.

How To Pick Your Facebook Fan Page Name

There are two theories for how you should choose a Facebook fan page name.

1. Simple Naming

Use your company, blog or personal name. Plain and simple. This helps build your brand and looks the most professional.

2. Descriptive Naming

Descriptive naming is where you name your fan page in a way that will attract attention to what you do. For example, "***How To Make Money Online With Tom Corson-Knowles***."

This way, when you post or when others share your content or mention your fan page, it shows up with your descriptive name - making it more likely for Facebook users to click it, come to your page and become your fan. It can also increase the number of fans who opt-in for your free report and join your email list.

Descriptive naming is especially powerful if you enjoy commenting, sharing and interacting on Facebook - because every time you do so your Fan Page name is being seen by potential customers in their newsfeeds.

Which naming strategy should you use?

Basically, I recommend using the simple naming strategy for most businesses. If you're a very social person and love to comment and interact on Facebook and are building your own personal brand then it may be better to use the descriptive naming strategy in order to display quickly who you are and how you help your customers.

STEP 3

Next, upload a photo for your fan page. I highly recommend uploading a photo of a person – either yourself or some of your employees. This is the photo people will be seeing in their news feeds and people on Facebook would much rather interact with a person than a brand – so make your fan page personable with a nice picture!

STEP 4.

Fill out the About section of your fan page and your website. This section is indexed by Google so it's important for Search Engine Optimization (SEO) as well as telling your fans and customers what you do. I recommend filling it out briefly to start with and then spend some time later on revamping it. Check out other popular fan pages to see how they are using the About section to promote their business.

Tip: Because the About section is indexed by Google, make sure to include any keywords you would like to rank for. For example, if you sell doorknobs, make sure to include the keyword doorknobs in your About section.

Now you've done all the basic work of setting up your fan page and you can go ahead and post your first status update!

ADVANCED FAN PAGE SETUP

After you've posted your first status update, let's complete all the details of maximizing your fan page for business.

STEP 1. UPLOAD A TIMELINE COVER PHOTO

Again, just like with your personal profile, you'll need to upload a Timeline cover photo. Remember, the dimensions of a cover photo should be 851 pixels wide x 315 or larger (because Facebook will automatically crop it).

STEP 2. EDIT PAGE SETTINGS

At the very top of your fan page, click "Edit Page" and then "Update Info."

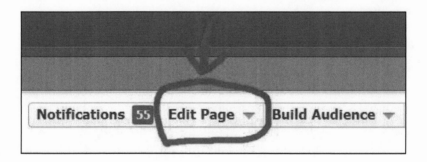

Depending on what type of fan page you have there will be different boxes in your info section. I recommend you fill out as much information as possible in each section to help your fans and customers learn more about you. Try to make your page info as descriptive and helpful as possible.

Make sure to include a link to your business website!

FAN PAGE RESOURCES

If there's anything you need help with, check out the resources section for Fan Page owners. When you're on the Update Info section of your fan page, just go to the left toolbar and click "Resources."

GETTING LIKES AND SETTING UP A VANITY URL

Now that you've filled out all your Facebook info, click "Like" on your fan page to become the first fan!

Next, invite your Facebook friends to like your page by clicking "Build Audience" at the top of your page and then "Invite Friends."

You can then select which of your friends to invite to like your fan page. I recommend inviting all of your friends! This will help you get as many fans as possible.

Also, you need to get 25 fans to set up a Vanity URL which is basically a unique URL just for your page that makes it easier for customers to find you on Facebook. This is especially important if you will be promoting your Fan Page at a physical location (on your product packaging or in your stores).

For example, my Vanity URL for my fan page is

www.facebook.com/TomCorsonKnowlesFanClub

way because *www.facebook.com/tomcorsonknowles* goes to my personal profile and was already taken.

The best Vanity URL to choose is one that is simple, easy to spell and easy to remember, preferably the name of your business. For example, facebook.com/yourbusiness. That way, you can promote your Vanity URL for your fan page and make it easier for your customers to find you on Facebook.

AWESOME TRICK! HOW TO LINK YOUR FAN PAGE TO YOUR PERSONAL PROFILE

This amazing trick allows you to link to your fan page straight from your Facebook profile in your "Works at..." section.

STEP 1. CLICK THE ABOUT SECTION OF YOUR PROFILE

About

🗂 **Kindle Publisher, Author, Speaker at Tom Corson-Knowles and Sales Coordinator at National Safety Associates, Inc.**

🎓 **Studied Online Marketing at How to Make Money Online with Tom Corson-Knowles**
Past: Peak Potentials and Enlightened Warrior Training Camp

STEP 2. CLICK "EDIT"

STEP 3. TYPE IN YOUR FAN PAGE

In the "Where did you work?" box, simply type in the name of your fan page and click it. Now your profile will display that you currently work at your fan page and anyone who clicks that will be taken to your fan page!

You can also use this neat trick for your education. In the box that says "Where did you go to college/university?" again just type in your fan page.

CHAPTER 5
FACEBOOK MARKETING STRATEGY – THE STEP-BY-STEP SYSTEM

CR80

OR MOST small businesses, making money with Facebook requires building the right system.

Unless you have a brand like Coca-Cola with billions of people around the world who consume your product regularly and pretty much everyone in the world knows who you are, you have to create a system that will allow you to capture new leads and turn those leads into customers.

You can't afford just to "advertise" on Facebook without actually generating leads and sales because you'll run out of money advertising sooner or later if you're not generating sales.

The bad news is you'll have to develop a system that makes Facebook profitable. The good news is it's much easier than you think!

All you have to do is set up a "marketing funnel" on Facebook where you get your fans and prospects to request more information and then you build the relationship and turn your fans into paying customers.

HOW TO CREATE A SALES FUNNEL

For those of you who understand online marketing and building a sales funnel, this will be super easy. If you're not familiar with building a sales funnel, then it'll be a little bit of a learning curve but I think you'll find it incredibly intuitive and easy to understand.

A sales funnel is basically the system or series of steps your prospects must go through in order to become a paying customer.

STEP 1. TRAFFIC

Above is a diagram of a simplified sales funnel. At the top of the funnel we have a very broad segment of prospects – for example, all of your Facebook fans, or, even broader, everyone who sees your Fan Page.

How do you get traffic on Facebook?

There are many ways to get traffic including using Facebook ads, posting regular status updates, interacting on Facebook, and building your fan base through your other websites and in your stores. We'll talk about how to use Facebook Ads in the next chapter.

Regular Status Updates

Posting regular status updates (at least one or two a day) is the easiest and most effective way to attract new fans and keep your old fans coming back for more. It's also free! Even if you spend millions of dollars on ads, no one cares if you don't post regular status updates so make sure you do that.

Get Fans From Your Website

If you have a website make sure you put a Facebook Like Box on the sidebar of your site so that your visitors can like your fan page with one click.

You can get a Like Box here from Facebook:

developers.facebook.com/docs/reference/plugins/like-box/

I also recommend you use Facebook Comments on your website and the Facebook like button for your web pages. If you use Wordpress, you can simply install the Facebook For Wordpress Plugin:

developers.facebook.com/wordpress/

If you don't use Wordpress for your site, then you can have your webmaster install Facebook comments for you.

Interacting on Facebook

If you love sharing and social media or are just naturally an outgoing person then you can attract new fans by joining conversations on Facebook. You can join groups, help answer questions on other fan pages and share new ideas with others in your industry.

If you're going to use this strategy, make sure to use Facebook as your fan page rather than as your personal profile so that when people see your posts, they see it was written by your fan page and can then like your page.

To do that, simply click the tiny arrow at the top right of the screen next the home button and pick which fan page you would like to use Facebook as.

Once you click your fan page, you will be commenting and sharing on Facebook as your fan page.

STEP 2. CAPTURING LEADS

But we know just because someone visits our fan page doesn't mean they're going to buy from us right now. So what we do is send them to a lead capture page or "squeeze page" as many online marketers call it.

On your lead capture page you ask for the prospects' name and email address so they can get more information about you and your products (and so you can market to them on a regular basis).

Here's an example of one of my lead capture pages if you've never seen one:

www.blogbusinessschool.com/

Generally, you want to offer something that your potential customers will see as very valuable and you want to offer it for free in return for your prospect's name and email. Examples of free products include a sample, an eBook, a training video or series of videos or a free consultation, just to name a few. Offering something for free does several good things for your business.

First, it will dramatically increase the number of new leads you get.

Second, it will increase goodwill with your prospects because they will be happy they got something valuable for free.

Third, it deepens your relationship with your prospects because they get to experience your free product before they make the decision to become a paying customer.

You can create your own Capture Pages and landing pages on Facebook using the Static Iframe app (it's free):

apps.facebook.com/iframehost/

You will need to know basic html to build a landing page on Facebook or have your web designer do it. Alternatively, you can redirect traffic from your Facebook landing page to one of your website landing pages. To do that, just click "redirect" once you've set up your iFrame tab.

STEP 3. MAKE OR DELIVER YOUR OFFER

After the prospect opts in to your email list for more information, it's now time to either deliver the information you promised or to make an offer to buy one of your products.

Often, online marketers will make what's called a "one time offer" (OTO) immediately after a prospect opts in. In this one time offer, you might offer your product at a discount or a bundle package at a discount. OTOs are especially effective when using advertising because the immediate sales generate by an OTO can either offset the costs of your advertising or completely pay for the cost of the ads.

STEP 4. FOLLOW UP, FOLLOW UP, FOLLOW UP

> *"Follow up, follow up, follow up until they buy... or die!"*
> **Tom Hopkins**

Once they've opted in to your email list, they can either buy from you or unsubscribe – because you're going to continually follow up with them as long as they give you permission to!

If someone opts in to your email list it means they have at least some interest in your products and services so it's your job to help them get what they want.

Depending on your business, you may want to follow up with these prospects with a new email once a week, once a day or once a month.

THAT'S IT!

That's really all there is to building a sales funnel – at least the basics of it. Once you've got your sales funnel set up and capturing leads and following up with them you will start to see REAL SALES being generated from Facebook. Without a funnel, it's very difficult to monetize Facebook and make it profitable.

CHAPTER 6
EVERYTHING YOU NEED TO KNOW ABOUT FACEBOOK ADS

ॐ

O KAY NOW you've got your Facebook sales funnel set up – congratulations!

It's now time to learn how to use Facebook Ads to explode your online sales and increase your number of Facebook fans at the same time.

HOW TO SET UP FACEBOOK ADS

The first step to setting up Facebook ads is to go to :

www.facebook.com/advertising

Once there, you can click "Create an Ad" at the top right of the page or call the number on the screen to get a personalized walkthrough on how to set up your Facebook Ads account if you're brand new to Facebook Ads.

CREATING AN AD

Once your Facebook Ads account is set up, just click Create an Ad or go to

www.facebook.com/ads/create/

Next, you will see a screen that looks like the picture below.

WHAT TO ADVERTISE

Now it's time to decide where you want people to go once they click on your ad. Do you want them to go to your fan page, a landing page on Facebook or to a website outside of Facebook?

Note: Facebook wants to maximize their revenue so they prefer ads that click through and remain within Facebook (for example, to your fan page). Thus, if you run a Facebook ads campaign to your Facebook landing page or fan page, it will cost much less than a Facebook ad campaign to your website outside of Facebook.

WHAT YOU CAN ADVERTISE

Facebook allows your ads to click through to your fan page, landing pages on your fan page, any other website outside of Facebook or a Facebook App.

Facebook also allows you to pay for Sponsored Stories and Promoted Posts. Let's cover standard ads first.

STANDARD FACEBOOK ADS

If you have a landing page set up already using the Static iFrame app or another similar free Facebook App, then you must first find the URL of your app and copy and paste that URL into the box that says "Choose a Facebook destination or enter a URL."

Next, you should see a screen that looks like this.

Now just fill in your headline (up to 25 characters), the text of your ad (up to 90 characters) and the image for your ad. I highly recommend setting up at least 10 ads to start with using different pictures, headlines and ad text to see which ones convert best for you and provide the highest Return On Investment (ROI).

Note: If possible, include a call to action in your ad such as "Click Like below for free tips." Facebook ads, unlike any other online ad in the world, do not charge you when a customer clicks "like" below the ad. This means that you can theoretically get 10 new fans for your fan page but only pay for 1 click if 10 people click "like" and only 1 person clicks on the ad. Having a call to action asking people to like the ad will increase the number of "free likes" you get from your advertising.

Next, there will be a Sponsored Stories section that looks like this:

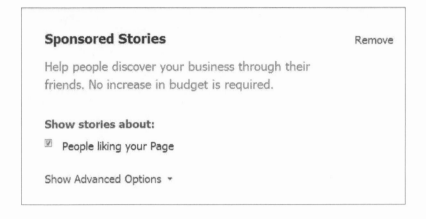

I recommend you click "remove" and not worry about sponsored stories right now – just focus on a basic ad to start so that you can more easily measure your ROI and get a feel for Facebook advertising.

CHOOSE YOUR AUDIENCE

Next, it's time to choose your audience. First, location!

LOCATION

You can choose the location of people who see your ads by country, state, city or even zip code.

Obviously, if you're a local business I would recommend ONLY advertising to people that live in your city and maybe the surrounding city. Otherwise, you'll end up paying for ads to people who can't buy from you because they live too far away.

If you sell products mostly online and have a national business, then just select the entire United States or whatever country you want to target.

For my online business, I do business internationally and so I advertise to people in the United States, United Kingdom, Australia and Canada. Why? Because they all speak English, have high average incomes compared with other countries and are likely to buy from me.

Note: The cost of your ads will vary drastically depending on what countries you advertise to. For example, the average cost of a click in Mexico may be 10 cents whereas it may be 50 cents or more in the United States.

Other factors that influence the cost of your ads include how targeted they are and the Click-Through Rate (CTR).

WHAT IS CTR?

Click-through rate or CTR is the ratio of how many times your ads are clicked compared to how many times they are seen by a potential customer. For example, if your ad is seen 1000 times (called impressions) and the ad gets clicked 10 times, that's a 1% CTR (which is very good for Facebook).

The higher your CTR, the cheaper your ads will be. The more targeted your ads, the higher your CTR. So it makes a lot of sense to target your ads as best you can to increase the number of clicks and reduce your cost of advertising!

AGE

Generally, I recommend never advertising to anyone younger than 25 or older than 65 unless your business specifically targets younger or older customers. This is because if you advertise to very young people (especially 13-18) they just don't have any spending money and probably won't buy from you (unless you sell cool stuff!).

Likewise, older customers over age 65 may be a bit out of date unless you offer something specifically for the older generation.

Targeting age is important – think carefully about it and see what age groups convert best for you.

GENDER

You can choose men, women or all. I recommend separating your ads between men and women and seeing which convert better – remember to test your ads!

Ads that use picture of women when advertising to women or men when advertising to men tend to convert better because of identification (customers identify with the picture and are more likely to buy because of it).

PRECISE INTERESTS

This is what separates Facebook ads from all other ads in the universe. Facebook has more information about its users' interests, information and values than any other entity in the world!

Because people fill out their Facebook profiles with information from where they live to what movies and fan pages they like, you can precisely target your ideal customer on Facebook in a way you can't with any other type of ad in the world.

Let's say you have a coffee business. Did you know that over 13 million people in the United States have a Facebook profile in which they mention they like coffee?

Well if you have a coffee business and want to advertise you can specifically target only people who already said they like coffee! This will not only increase your sales but it will save you money because you won't have to waste advertising dollars on people like me who hate coffee!

BROAD CATEGORIES

Broad categories basically use looser information when putting together the advertising group. So for example, the "Computer programming" group in broad categories doesn't just include people who like computer programming – it also includes people who MIGHT like computer programming based on their similar interests (like maybe software or something).

I never recommend using broad categories – it's the lazy person's approach to Facebook ads. Always use specific categories and you'll get higher CTR and a higher ROI on your ads.

CONNECTIONS

Connections allows you to advertise to people based on whether or not they are already connected to your fan page or personal profile. This can be handy if you only want to advertise to new clients and don't want to advertise to your Facebook friends and current fans.

You can also advertise JUST to your current fans which is a great strategy if you have a special offer or sale because they are more likely to click on it and buy from you and this will reduce your advertising costs for such a promotion.

FRIENDS OF CONNECTIONS

This allows you to target people who are friends of your fan page or profile. This is great because if you advertise to a friend of your current fan, the ad will say "John (their friend) likes this" and gives you social proof that your fan page is cool.

I always recommend advertising to friends of connections if you already have at least 1000 fans. Otherwise, you don't have enough fans to make this option work well for you so just ignore it.

NEW CAMPAIGN NAME

Here you can create a new Facebook ads campaign or click "Use Existing Campaign" to use a campaign that you've already set up.

I recommend using separate campaigns for separate fan pages, websites or applications.

CAMPAIGN BUDGET

Here you can set your daily or lifetime budget for your ad campaign.

CAMPAIGN SCHEDULE

I generally run my ads continuously unless it's for a short-term promotion – then you can just cancel or pause the ads when the promotion has ended.

PRICING

I highly recommend using CPC for new advertisers rather than CPM advertising. CPC means "cost per click" and you pay each time someone clicks your ad. CPM means "cost per mil" which means you pay for every 1000 impressions (regardless of if anyone clicks your ad).

Start with CPC ads for sure. I never use CPM and I don't recommend it because 90% of the time it will cost more than CPC.

AUDIENCE

Once you've filled out all the info for your ad targeting and pricing, check the "Audience" on the right side of the ad page.

For most businesses, I recommend targeting an audience of a minimum of 10,000 people. If your audience is much smaller then you will likely get very little exposure and clicks.

However, if you own a local business in a small town, your audience might be smaller than 10,000 and that's okay – it's not worth expanding the geography of your ads to reach people who can't buy from you.

I also recommend advertising to less than 1 million people if possible – because if your audience is too big then you're not targeting your ads enough and your CTR is likely to be low (although this is not always the case, it's just a general rule of thumb).

SPONSORED STORIES

There's another ad type available called "Sponsored Stories" and they appear on the right side of a user's profile just like Facebook Ads. The stories link to one of your status updates on your fan page.

Sponsored stories are mostly used by big brands and I highly recommend you never use them. Why?

Because tests have been done by SEOmoz and myself that have shown sponsored stories cost way more than a Promoted Post and get much less engagement. This is because Promoted posts appear in the news feed NOT as an ad.

PROMOTE A POST

Promoting a Facebook post can be a very powerful tool for gaining massive amounts of traffic and engagement with a very small budget. When you promote a post it will be seen by more of your fans and friends of your fans in their news feed. The only difference is that the post will say "sponsored" on the right side of the post next to where it says "Share".

You can promote a post on your fan page by clicking "Promote" underneath the post and selecting your budget for the promotion. Promoted posts are currently only available to fan pages with 500 or more fans. You can only promote a post if you already have your

Facebook Ads account setup with a credit card. You can setup your ads account at:

www.facebook.com/ads

Once you've promoted your post you can see how many views the post has received that you paid for, how many it got organically (if you hadn't promoted it at all) and how many you received virally (as a result of paid traffic liking, commenting and sharing).

I recommend using Promoted posts for content that is likely to be viral. For example, if you're offering a free report or free product sample that your fans will probably love to receive then this is the perfect occasion to Promote the post announcing the free stuff. People love getting stuff for free so they will share it, like and comment if they appreciate what you're sharing.

I do not recommend promoting every post on Facebook – that can end up costing you a lot of money. Preferably, you want to promote posts that a) offer something for sale so you can monetize it or b) give something away for free or c) are likely to viral so that you can benefit from the additional viral traffic.

FACEBOOK ADS RECAP

So there you have it!

Now you know how to set up your Facebook ads and not to use Sponsored Stories (instead use a Promoted post!).

Now it's time to discover how to use the brand new Facebook Offers to get some great exposure and ROI on your advertising budget.

CHAPTER 7
NEW FACEBOOK OFFERS

ACEBOOK INITIALLY launched Offers initially only for local businesses but they can now be used by any fan page with 400 or more fans.

A Facebook Offer is basically like a coupon people can opt in for. When the Facebook user accepts the offer, they get an email from Facebook with a link to your site that contains the coupon or offer information.

The sky is the limit for your use of Facebook Offers. Let me show you some of my favorite uses.

1. FREE STUFF!

Everyone loves free stuff! I'm sure you're tired of reading that by now – but this strategy works extremely well on Facebook.

For example, if you're an ice cream shop and give away a free sample of ice cream or buy 1 get one free ice cream cone, your offer will do very well on Facebook.

Since I sell mostly information products, training and services, I love to give away free reports, courses and video trainings using a Facebook Offer because every time I do it turns me a profit.

Just don't overuse Facebook Offers and post them every day – your fans will get tired of just seeing offers from you. It should be just for "special occasions" so that your fans are getting lots of great content from you on a daily basis in addition to some great offers every few weeks or so.

2. DISCOUNT / COUPON

A discount or coupon offer can be great for some businesses. Maybe you've got a $97 product and want to offer it to your fans at a special fan-only discount.

You can set up a coupon code on your website and give the code only to people who register for the offer on Facebook.

3. PRODUCT LAUNCH

If you're launching a new product then it's the perfect time for a Facebook offer! Why not introduce your new product to tens of thousands or hundreds of thousands of people on Facebook?

Product launches are great because you can use the word NEW in your offer – people love new stuff! Especially if it's a great product.

Facebook Offers are now a part of the marketing mix for every single product launch I do – and I recommend you use it the same way.

CHAPTER 8
THINGS TO AVOID

જી

I HAD to include a chapter on things to avoid doing on Facebook. Mostly because I see a lot of people making these mistakes (or they're mistakes I used to make but learned not to the hard way).

It's not just important that you know what to do to grow your business on Facebook – it's also important to know what NOT to do so you don't get bad press or, even worse, your Facebook page taken down for violating the Terms of Service (TOS).

DON'T SPAM

Now maybe you're not a spammer – that's a good thing! But wait until your new product launches and you're so excited to tell everyone on Facebook and get a notification that you've been spamming.

Hey – it happens to all of us (at least it's happened to me and many others I've spoken to about Facebook marketing).

WHAT FACEBOOK CONSIDERS SPAMMING

Basically, if you post the same message on more than 4 or 5 fan pages you will probably be flagged for spam.

Anyone can click "report spam" on any comment or post on Facebook – so if you rack up enough of those in a short period, Facebook could penalize your account for spamming.

Luckily, you won't get banned the first time (unless it's just an egregious case of super spam but I've never seen it happen to anyone).

Basically, if you post on other fan pages, groups or walls repeatedly and other Facebook users report your comments or posts as spam, you can get punished by Facebook. Usually, they will just disable your ability to post on other peoples' fan pages for a few days.

Just make sure that when you're posting on other fan pages you're posting something useful and helpful and not just promoting your own products.

DON'T JUST TRY TO SELL STUFF

Facebook is a social community and your fans are normal people just like you and me. They don't want to constantly see sales offers in their news feeds – they want to hear something NEW! That's why it's called a NEWS feed!

So share exciting, interesting, funny and creative status updates, pictures, videos and a variety of posts that keep your fans entertained. This will dramatically improve your EdgeRank and increase the number of people who see your sales offers on Facebook.

If you want to kill your EdgeRank fast, just post sales offers 7 days in a row and you'll see your fan engagement tank. Or you can learn from this book and never make that mistake!

BE CONSISTENT!

You'd be amazed how many businesses don't take Facebook marketing seriously. So they post once a day for a while and then go on vacation and no one is managing the fan page. Little do they know their customers are asking questions on the fan page and no one is helping them!

Make sure someone is checking your fan page on a daily basis and responding to your fans and customers as well as posting interesting content for you fans. ALWAYS be consistent – it's the key to marketing.

Remember, it takes 7-13 marketing exposures before a prospect becomes a customer. The more you expose your fans to your status updates on a daily basis, the more sales you will generate over time – guaranteed.

CHAPTER 9
FACEBOOK APPS

ᘓᘒ

F ACEBOOK APPS provide an entirely new way to engage with potential customers and prospects. For example, Zynga, the creator of Farmville and other Facebook Games, is now a publicly traded company and it all started with a Facebook App.

You can hire someone to create a Facebook App for your business. For example, some entrepreneurs are promoting video games for business Facebook fan pages to provide more fan engagement and attract new customers.

Personally, I'm not a fan of putting games on my fan page. I'd rather provide education, inspiration and useful information for my fans and customers – but it's up to you.

There are also Facebook Apps you can use on your fan page for many other purposes besides games.

HELPFUL FACEBOOK APPS FOR BUSINESS

Below are some of the most useful Facebook Apps I've found for small businesses.

STATIC IFRAME APP

Static Iframe App allows you to create Facebook landing pages, fan gates, and redirects to any 3rd party website. This is the standard app I use for almost every Facebook fan page because it's free and so versatile if you know a little bit of HTML (or you can hire someone for a few dollars to set it up for you).

It's available at:

www.apps.facebook.com/iframehost

FACEBOOK FAN REVIEWS

The Facebook Fan Reviews app allows your customers to leave reviews and testimonials directly on your Facebook Fan Page and the reviews are then posted to their personal profile so all their friends can see.

This is a great way to gather testimonials, reviews and get lots of viral traffic and referrals through Facebook.

You can also install the Facebook Fan Reviews app on your website, sales pages and blog to give more social proof to your business and make your customers feel more comfortable buying from you.

You can get Facebook Fan Reviews at:

www.juicetom.smashitsoc.hop.clickbank.net

TOP FANS

The Top Fans app displays the top fans on your fan page based on how often they comment, like and share your posts. This can be a great way to reward your top fans and "challenge" your fans to engage with your page more.

You can get Top Fans at:

www.facebook.com/mytopfans

Pinterest Page App

The Pinterest Page App displays your most recent pins from Pinterest. This is a great app if you have a very visual business (like selling art or merchandise) and you have an active Pinterest marketing campaign as well.

You can get Pinterest Page App at:

www.woobox.com/pinterest

Shopping Cart Apps

There are several apps you can use to sell products directly on your Facebook fan page.

Ecwid

Ecwid is a free shopping cart designed for use on any Facebook page or website. Ecwid supports drag-and-drop customization, allows you to mirror your Facebook cart onto any website, and also provided a single Web-based management interface for all carts you display. Ecwid currently has over 60,000 monthly active users.

You can get Ecwid at:

www.facebook.com/ecwid

Payvment

This Facebook e-commerce solution lets users add a professional-grade storefront to a Facebook page. The app provides an admin area built directly into Facebook to manage your storefront, products and sales. Payvment currently has over 350,000 users Facebook users.

You can get Payvment at:

www.facebook.com/payvment

BIGCOMMERCE

The BigCommerce SocialShop app lets online sellers and merchants add a Shop tab to a Facebook Business or Fan page. Through the tab, Facebook users can browse products and buy through Facebook. The service is free for 15-days with basic pricing starting at $24.95 per month. BigCommerce currently has over 35,000 monthly active users.

You can get BigCommerce at:

on.fb.me/13mI58q

VENDORSHOP

VendorShop is a free ecommerce shopping cart that lets users setup an online shop tab on any Facebook page. Once the VendorShop application is installed you can add products and prices. A PayPal checkout service is used for payments. VendorShop currently has over 32,000 monthly active users.

You can get VendorShop at:

www.facebook.com/Vendorshop

MUNCOM

Muncom is a free PHP shopping cart that lets you create a cart to display on your Facebook profile or Facebook Business Page. To create the cart you need to first design a free store on Muncom.com. Muncom's shopping cart service is currently in beta and the Facebook application has over 2,500 monthly active users.

You can get Muncom at:

www.facebook.com/ecommercecart

CHAPTER 10
FACEBOOK ANALYTICS

 C3℘

F ACEBOOK ANALYTICS is a very new field. Despite how large Facebook has become, only a few companies provide useful Analytics for Facebook.

This is because Facebook has its own Analytics platform called Facebook Insights which is available for all fan page owners.

FACEBOOK INSIGHTS

You can access Facebook Insights for your fan page by clicking the "See All" button next to the Insights box on your fan page management panel.

HOW TO USE FACEBOOK INSIGHTS

When you first sign in to Facebook Insights, you will see a graph that shows you how many posts you've made each day, how many people were talking about your fan page and your weekly total reach. All this data is okay but it's not extremely helpful.

So scroll down and look at each of your posts individually to see how they've been doing. You'll see a table like this:

Look specifically at the "Virality" indicator on the right side which will be a percent. Notice some of my posts had as high as 34.33% virality while another one had only 0.48% virality – that's a huge difference!

Virality is an important indicator because it tells you how many people saw that post because someone shared it with them or liked it. This is huge! The higher the virality of your posts, the more exposure you will get and the more money you will make.

Take a look at your posts and notice which ones are getting very high virality and which ones have a very low virality. Then simply learn from your data and continue posting content that your fans love and stop posting stuff that they don't respond to.

It sounds simple (and it really is) but you'd be amazed how many people don't even look at their Facebook Insights to see how their posts are doing! If you do this one thing, you will stand out from the competition because you won't be posting blindly anymore – you'll know what your fans love even before you post it.

Next, click the "Likes" button on the top left of your Insights tab and you'll see a breakdown of your fans by gender and age. This can be important depending on your business – are you attracting more male or female fans? What age groups are most likely to connect with your message and brand?

This is all great research for marketing!

Under the chart, you'll see a list of what countries your fans are from, cities and what languages they speak. This can be especially important if you do business internationally.

Remember, Facebook now allows you to target your fan page posts based on location of your fans and even the language they speak so you can target different posts to different countries and languages.

Scroll down just a bit more on the Likes tab and you'll see a chart that says "Where Your Likes Come From" which shows you how your new fans liked your page. This can help you track where your fans are coming from. Is it from a like box on your website, from Facebook Ads or from a viral post you shared?

This is all great information!

THIRD PARTY FACEBOOK ANALYTICS

There are third party Facebook Analytics sites that will give you different kinds of data about your fans and fan engagement but I haven't personally found any that are worth the price.

Unless you have over 50,000 fans or so, I wouldn't even bother thinking about using a third-party analytics company because it's very unlikely you'll see a positive return on that investment until your fan base is very large.

Bonus Resources

❧

Daily Facebook Fan Page Checklist

1. Check your messages and respond to any new messages from fans.

2. Check your notifications and respond to any relevant comments on your posts.

3. Check your wall and respond to any new posts from fans.

4. Post at least 1 interesting, educational or entertaining picture for you fans. Looking for interesting photos? Search for other fan pages in your industry or a related industry that have more fans than you do and see what images they have posted that are getting tons of shares, likes and comments. Then just download the picture and upload it to your fan page.

5. Post at least one interesting quote, question or piece of advice for your fans. Looking for content? Search for quotes online if you're not sure what else to do.

Special Facebook Group

Come join our Facebook group just for readers like you who want to take their Facebook marketing to the next level. In this group we'll be sharing our successes, marketing tips and strategies with each other so that we can all continue to grow our businesses on Facebook.

This is also a fantastic group for finding joint venture partners and cross-promotion opportunities! Imagine if you had hundreds of other Facebook Fan Page owners collaborating with you – imagine how big of an impact you could have.

It's also a great place to get any questions you have answered as well.

Come join us on Facebook at:

www.facebook.com/groups/BusinessOwnersBook

FREE BLOGGING FOR BUSINESS TRAINING

‿ෂ∞

I F YOU'RE a business owner and want to learn how to start a blog for your business that makes a profit, I've developed a free online training program to teach you everything from how to build your blog to getting traffic to monetizing it.

You can get the free training at:

www.BlogBusinessSchool.com

FREE TWITTER TRAINING

CS&O

TO THANK you for buying this book I want to give you my best-selling book on How To Make Money With Twitter as a special bonus.

I've been using Twitter for years to get hundreds of new leads a month for my online businesses and it's a great way to promote your books in very little time once you set the system up.

You can grab your free copy here:

bit.ly/MlNne2

MOTIVATIONAL VIDEOS

CRANO

I HOPE this book has been motivational for you - but I also know you might not read this book every single day.

So I'd like to share some inspiring videos with you to keep you motivated on your book marketing journey. You can watch them anytime you want to get motivated and stay motivated to make positive changes in your life.

I know these videos have helped me stay inspired, motivated and passionate – and I hope they help you too!

You might not like all of these videos – that's okay! Just watch the ones that resonate with you and make you feel good. If it works for you keep it. If it doesn't just throw it out!

Life Changing Motivational Video!! So Inspiring!

www.youtube.com/watch?v=Yxigy8HngvE

Best Motivational Video Scenes Ever Made! Inspiring

www.youtube.com/watch?v=KRXP-EKgMiw

The Greatest Inspirational Speech Ever Made by Charlie Chaplin (Motivation!)

www.youtube.com/watch?v=14pLwX107kE

The Motivational Speaker With No Arms and No Legs - Nick Vujicic

www.youtube.com/watch?v=YpaSZOq0C3U

How Bad Do You Want It? Success! Motivational Video Part 2

www.youtube.com/watch?v=0b1nCMIU2bM

Motivation! There Are No Limitations! Inspirational Video

www.youtube.com/watch?v=lQdi-TgCaxU

40 Inspirational and Motivational Speeches in 2 Minutes

www.youtube.com/watch?v=obJiTFKmNI4

Muhammad Ali Inspirational Speech (Cassius Clay Boxing Motivation)

www.youtube.com/watch?v=dGk0R63C0eM

I am a champion the greatest speech ever ENG SUB

www.youtube.com/watch?v=fBZ-DLhISEE

Success: How Bad Do You Want It? Inspirational Video!

www.youtube.com/watch?v=IG1vac3TZ_Q

The Best Motivational Workout Video Ever!!

www.youtube.com/watch?v=49jD9AbITyg

Best Motivational Video For Startups And Entrepreneurs

www.youtube.com/watch?v=8NxDO6fA5rU

Winning Is A Habit! Best Motivational Video Ever!!

www.youtube.com/watch?v=U1hkzCK03tI

Truly The Best Motivational Video Ever! So Inspirational

www.youtube.com/watch?v=MLVHYlO6oso

The Best Motivational Video Ever - Don't Quit On Me Brock!!

www.youtube.com/watch?v=fOyiSEonUFA

Excerpt From '57 Hot Business Marketing Strategies'

❦

Strategy 11. Guest Blogging

As long as you have a website or something you're selling online, guest blogging can be an incredibly powerful marketing strategy. The best thing is that it's 100% free!

Searching for the Right Blogs

To start with guest blogging, you want to search for other blogs in your niche OR in niches that are similar or compatible with yours so that you can build a relationship with them and share your info with their audience.

For example, if you have a blog about dog training, you could search for blogs about dogs, or blogs about dog training, or blogs about cats and cat training (you could write an article for them about dogs vs. cats - the never-ending debate!).

The key here is to think of AS MANY different types of niches that you could fit into and add value to, and that would add value to you as well.

Just remember to be open-minded - maybe horse training blogs would like you to write an article for them about the top 5 things you learned as a dog trainer and how that could be applied to horses. Be creative and you will find many more opportunities for collaboration, guest blogging and building links to your site.

Once you've picked your search term, let's say it's "dog training" for now, you're going to add blog to the end of that term. So you would go to Google.com, type in "dog training blog" and hit search!

CLICK AND ANALYZE

At first, this step will take you a bit of time because you're just starting to learn how blogs work and how to navigate other peoples' sites.

Here are some general tips to make figuring out which sites to contact and which sites to ignore a whole lot easier:

First, if it's a news site, throw it out. For example, if you see well.blogs.newyorktimes.com in the search results, just skip past it - because I don't think the New York Times is going to accept your guest post... yet!

Second, if it's a duplicate site, only click one of them. Sometimes, Google will give you the same domain name several times in a search - so just click one of them and skip the extras. For example, you may see the following sites in the search results:

> well.blogs.nytimes.com

> business.blogs.nytimes.com

> science.blogs.nytimes.com

If you see search results with several links from one domain there's no reason to click all of those links from the same website so just click one of them and move down the list until you find a link to a new domain.

Third, ignore spam blogs and low quality sites!

Here's a good example:

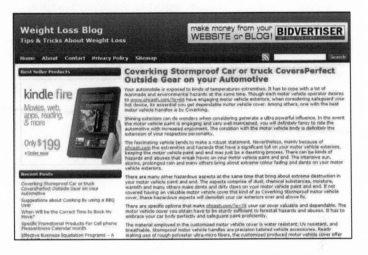

This site has a Google PageRank 2 - MUST BE A GREAT SITE TO GET A LINK FROM, RIGHT?

No way! Its Alexa rank is 15041954 - that means there are more than 15 million sites getting more traffic than that site - meaning it's essentially a garbage site that Google gives no traffic - and neither should you!

Do NOT solicit sites like this for links - even if you got a link from that site, it would do you more harm than good because it's quite likely Google has penalized that site for being spam, selling links, duplicate content or some other blackhat tricks.

If the Alexa Rank alone wasn't enough to let you know that site was not worth contacting just look at the home page! It says it's a weight loss blog and the home page article is just a spam advertisement for a "Coverking Stormproof Car" filled with affiliate links and ads!

If you see a site like this, close it out immediately and move on! (Also, if you get contacted by someone offering to sell or trade links from a site like that just ignore them!)

Don't do business with spammers - it will do more harm than good and could destroy your precious reputation with Google, especially early on!

WHAT YOU'RE LOOKING FOR IN A GOOD BLOG

You're basically looking for quality sites with unique content that get traffic and are recognized by Google as being a legitimate, authoritative site.

Here are my general rules:

PAGERANK

The PageRank should be 1 or higher. When you're starting out, it's fine to guest post on lots of PR 1 or PR2 websites. As your blog grows in traffic, you may not have time to write for such sites and would want to write for PR 3 or higher sites (but it may take you a few months get to that point so be patient!).

WHAT IS GOOGLE PAGERANK?

Google PageRank is an indicator from 0 to 10 that tells you how much Google values a website in terms of its "authority." A site with a PageRank 0 has basically no authority (either because it's brand new or because it has no quality incoming links).

A site with a PageRank 10 has extremely high quality – and there are very few of them. Google and Twitter have PageRank 10. Facebook has a PageRank 9.

Contrary to what many SEO gurus will tell you, PageRank CANNOT tell you whether or not a site is worth getting a link from. Google now uses PageRank to "fool" SEO experts into thinking Google actually uses PageRank to determine search engine results – they don't!

For example, the spam site I showed you before with a PageRank 2 would NOT be worth getting a link from. In fact, if you had hundreds of links from sites like that, Google might even penalize your site.

This is why I only use PageRank as a general guide to whether or not a site is worth getting a link from – and I use other factors like the Alexa Rank and the site's own design and content to guide me.

ALEXA RANK

When you first start out, any site with an Alexa Rank of 1,000,000 or lower should be just fine for guest posting. Basically, if a site is in the top 1 million sites, it's probably a decent site (just make sure the site LOOKS like a legitimate website too and is not really a spam site like the example above).

WHAT IS ALEXA RANK?

Alexa is an independent website that monitors all the sites on the internet and ranks them in terms of their monthly, weekly and daily traffic and page views.

The Alexa Rank starts at 1 for the website with the most traffic in the world (currently Facebook) and counts up from there. Therefore, the lower your Alexa Rank, the better!

I use the Alexa Rank in conjunction with Google PageRank to make sure a site is legitimate and worthy of guest posting. For example, if a site has a Google PageRank 5 (A very nice, high PageRank) and an Alexa Rank of 12,231,221 (A very poor Alexa Rank), then I know something is amiss – it doesn't add up.

I would never solicit a link from a site like that because they are obviously using some kind of blackhat SEO techniques or they have been penalized by Google – either way, I want nothing to do with a site like that. And neither should you!

SITE LAYOUT AND CONTENT

The site needs to look human. If the only thing you see above the fold is Adsense ads in the header and sidebar, then it's probably a spam site. If it looks like a cookie-cutter website with no human elements to it, it's probably just junk.

If the site's domain is something like weightlossdieting.com but you actually look at the site and all the articles are about electronics, then it's probably a spam site. You want to make sure the site is "congruent" and that it actually looks like a legitimate website with useful information and that it's actively being managed by a real person.

Remember, you're looking for a site that looks like a **real person** actually manages it.

The Alexa Rank, Google PageRank and site design/content need to all be telling the same story – that this is a legitimate website with helpful information that gets a good amount of visitors on a daily basis. Otherwise, it's not worth getting a link from. Period.

QUESTIONABLE CONTENT

It pretty much goes without saying that you should avoid any sites that contain pornography, hate speech, illegal activities or anything that might shine a poor light on you and your business. Don't get caught up in trying to get links and forget that it's about quality first and quantity second!

Getting links from questionable sites will only hurt your traffic not help it.

Remember this before you ever hire someone else to build links to your website! Make sure you are reviewing the work they're doing and that they're not just sending spam links to your website. Many so-called SEO experts can do more harm than good when it comes to getting traffic to your site.

Contacting Bloggers

If the site looks like a real quality site, it's time to contact them!

Now you would be surprised but you will find many bloggers who have no way to contact them through their blog - they haven't listed their email address anywhere, there's no web form for contacting them, there's no "Contact Page," etc…

It's almost as if they don't want anyone to contact them!

These bloggers I just ignore - because if you can't find a way to contact them, chances are they aren't serious enough about blogging to waste your time trying to get in touch with them.

Most often, sites like this are free blogs hosted on blogger or wordpress (the URL ends with a blogger or wordpress such as example.blogger.com or example.wordpress.com)

There are 3 main ways a blogger will post their contact information:

#1. CONTACT

They will have a web page called Contact or Contact Us - just use your keyboard to search for "contact."

Neat Trick: Finding Text On A Web Page

On a PC you hit CTRL + F and type in the word you're searching for.

On a Mac, hit the Apple Command Button + F and type what you're searching for.

Either way, your computer will automatically find the letters or words you typed into the search box if they exist on the page.

If you don't see a contact page or form, then try to find the...

#2. ABOUT / ABOUT ME PAGE

Many times bloggers will have all their contact info in the About/About Me/About Us page of their site.

Just use that nifty search trick I taught you before and type in "about". If you don't see that, then try to find their contact info in the...

#3. SIDEBAR

Sometimes a blogger will list their contact info in the sidebar - so just look for it there if you can't find it elsewhere.

If that doesn't work, your last hope is...

#4. SOCIAL MEDIA

Some bloggers, either because they're tired of being spammed or they just don't know better, will only have their contact info for Twitter, a Facebook Fan Page or other social media accounts.

ou can send them a tweet or message on the social network and see if they respond!

If that doesn't work then it's time to...

#5. MOVE ON

If steps 1-4 don't work, then just move on!

There are plenty of other high quality bloggers who actually care enough about their blog readers to provide contact info - these are the bloggers you want to work with!

FOLLOWING THROUGH

When a blog owner responds to your message, follow through!

If they ask you to write an article, write it promptly and send it to them and make sure it meets their guidelines and specifications. Make sure it's a HELPFUL article and not just promoting your blog - it should add real value to anyone who reads it.

You can do all the promotion you want of your own blog and your work in your author bio beneath the guest post.

SEE GUEST POSTING IN ACTION

You can see one of my guest posts in action here to get a feel for what they look like:

ediblegoddess.com/2012/05/growing-your-own-fresh-produce-got-easier/

In this post, my author bio appears before the article begins (although most bloggers put the author bio underneath it).

Here's another example guest post where my author bio appears below the post in a nice Author Box:

socialmarketingwriting.com/5-reasons-guest-blogging-is-the-best-traffic-generator/

SAMPLE EMAIL TO BLOGGER:

If you're not sure what to write to a blogger for a first-time contact, try something similar to this:

Hi [Name],

I love your blog! It's always inspiring to see others like you who are sharing the message of [Your Niche] in an easy to understand and exciting way.

I'd love to see if there's some way we could collaborate with our sites through guest blogging, social media, or something else. I blog about [Your Niche] too. Check it out and let me know if you think it's a good fit. [Link To Your Site]

[Salutation],

[Your Name]

I always like to keep my emails short, sweet and to the point and customize them to the blogger I'm contacting. For example, if I notice an article on their site about their two adorable poodles, I might say "I love poodles too!" or something similar to let them know you actually read their blog.

WHAT NOT TO DO

Here's an actual email sent to me by some spammer. Don't write like this!

Honestly, if you can't even write an email with good grammar and spelling how could you possibly write a good guest post for someone?

HORRIBLY WRITTEN EMAIL WHICH YOU SHOULD NEVER EMULATE

"Hi,

I saw your blog it is interesting, i want to introduce myself as a guest blogger. I have some interesting topics and contents are written by me after a short research..

If you are interested let me know...Looking forward to write useful contents for your blog..

Regards,

John"

Thanks John! I'll be sure to let you know when I need horribly written articles for my blog.

CONTINUE THE RELATIONSHIP WITH THE BLOGGER

After you write a guest post for their site, maybe ask if they'd like to write a post for your site? Offer to help them in return.

Another great thing you should do when you guest post is to share the article you wrote in all of your social media channels – it helps promote their blog and it helps you too by showing your fans and followers that you're a credible authority, worthy of your articles being posted on other sites and blogs.

Always be creative and open to more ways to collaborate with other bloggers and website owners – we all win together if we help each other.

Don't just be a taker – be a giver too! Givers truly gain in the world of blogging.

[End of Excerpt]

If you enjoyed this marketing tip from *57 Hot Business Marketing Strategies,* you can grab your copy at:

www.Amazon.com/Author/Business

Connect With Tom

ﾟ৪৪ﾟ

T HANK YOU so much for taking the time to read this book. I'm excited for you to start your path to making the income of your dreams as a nonfiction author

If you have any questions of any kind, feel free to contact me directly at: *Tom@JuiceTom.com*

You can follow me on Twitter: *@JuiceTom*

And connect with me on Facebook: *on.fb.me/W8fA7B*

You can check out my internet marketing blog for the latest updates here: *bit.ly/V8iRox*

I'm wishing you the best of health, happiness and success!

Here's to you!

Tom Corson-Knowles

ABOUT THE AUTHOR

TOM CORSON-KNOWLES is the #1 Amazon best-selling author of *The Kindle Publishing Bible* and *How To Make Money With Twitter*, among others. He lives in Kapaa, Hawaii. Tom loves educating and inspiring other entrepreneurs to succeed and live their dreams.

Learn more at:

www.Amazon.com/author/business

OTHER BOOKS BY TOM CORSON-KNOWLES

ଓଃୠ

Secrets Of The Six-Figure Author: Mastering the Inner Game of Writing, Publishing and Marketing Books

amzn.com/B00D4B5NNQ

Systemize, Automate, Delegate: How to Grow a Business While Traveling, on Vacation and Taking Time Off

amzn.com/B00BTGD8RG

The Kindle Publishing Bible: How To Sell More Kindle eBooks On Amazon

amzn.com/B00A86QV9A

The Kindle Writing Bible: How To Write a Bestselling Nonfiction Book From Start To Finish

amzn.com/B00AXTNY9W

The Kindle Formatting Bible: How To Format Your Ebook For Kindle Using Microsoft Word

amzn.com/B00AHO9R1M

How To Make Money With Twitter

amzn.com/B008QFJTK8

The Blog Business Book: How To Start A Blog And Turn It Into A Six Figure Online Business

amzn.com/B009IV524Q

How To Reduce Your Debt Overnight: A Simple System To Eliminate Credit Card And Consumer Debt

amzn.com/B007QMHUR6

INDEX